THE OPEN DOOR BOOK OF POETRY
First published 2005
by New Island
2 Brookside
Dundrum Road
Dublin 14

www.newisland.ie

Copyright selection and editorial matter © 2005 Niall MacMonagle

The right of Niall MacMonagle to be identified as the editor of this
work has been asserted by him in accordance with the Copyright,
Designs and Patents Act, 1988

A CIP catalogue record for this book is available from the British Library

ISBN 1 904301 70 3

New Island receives financial assistance from
The Arts Council (An Chomhairle Ealaíon), Dublin, Ireland.

Typeset by New Island
Printed in Ireland by ColourBooks
Cover design by Artmark

1 3 5 4 2

Dear Reader,

On behalf of myself and the other contributing authors, I would like to welcome you to the Open Door series. We hope that you enjoy the books and that reading becomes a lasting pleasure in your life.

Warmest wishes,

Patricia Scanlan.

Patricia Scanlan
Series Editor

THE OPEN DOOR SERIES IS DEVELOPED WITH THE ASSISTANCE OF THE CITY OF DUBLIN VOCATIONAL EDUCATION COMMITTEE.

for
Sean and Lil MacMonagle
and in memory of
Molly Kirby
who loved, especially, the
poem on page fifty-one

Contents

Introduction   viii

Anonymous *Frankie and Johnny*   1

Anonymous *The Tortoise*   7

Anonymous *Western Wind*   9

William Blake *A Poison Tree*   11

Eavan Boland *This Moment*   13

Lucy Brennan *When All Is Said and Done*   15

Robert Burns *Auld Lang Syne*   17

Paddy Bushe *Tibetan Shepherd Boys*   21

Don Byrne *Ouzo Time*   23

George Gordon, Lord Byron *So We'll Go No More A-Roving*   25

C. P. Cavafy *The Mirror in the Hall*   27

Billy Collins *The Dead*   29

Padraic Colum *An Old Woman of the Roads*   30

Pádraig J. Daly *On the Rooftops: Rome 1970*   33

W. H. Davies *Leisure*   35

Greg Delanty *The Present*   37

Emily Dickinson *'"Hope" is the thing with feathers'*   39

Noel Duffy *Daisy-Chain*   40

Paul Durcan *The Cabinet Table*   43

U. A. Fanthorpe *BC : AD*   45

Thomas Hardy *Weathers*   47

Seamus Heaney *Mid-Term Break*   48

A. E. Housman *XXXVI* from *More Poems*   51

Pat Ingoldsby *More of Me*   53

Joe Kane *The Boy Who Nearly Won the
  Texaco Art Competition*   54

Patrick Kavanagh *Wet Evening in April*   57

Brendan Kennelly *Begin*   58

Nick Laird *Done*   61

Philip Larkin *The Trees*   63

Anne Le Marquand Hartigan *Cup*   65

Joan McBreen *Portrait of Parents and Child*   66

Paula Meehan *The Pattern*   69

Czeslaw Milosz *Gift*   75

Adrian Mitchell *Celia Celia*   77

Paul Muldoon *Why Brownlee Left*   79

John O'Donnell *Watching Stars*   80

Dennis O'Driscoll *Years After*   82

Grace Paley *I See My Friend Everywhere*   85

Linda Pastan *Marks*   87

Padraic Pearse *The Wayfarer*   89

Christina Rossetti *Remember*   91

Anne Sexton *Red Roses*   92

William Shakespeare *Sonnet 29*   95

Eileen Sheehan *Waking*   96

Henry Shukman *Snowy Morning*   98

Wole Soyinka *Telephone Conversation*   101

Stevie Smith *Not Waving but Drowning*   105

Alfred, Lord Tennyson *The Eagle*   107

Edward Thomas *Adlestrop*   109
William Wordsworth *'I Wandered Lonely as a Cloud'* 110
James Wright *A Blessing*   112
W. B. Yeats *The Lake Isle of Innisfree*   115
Acknowledgments   116

'Twice in your life you know that you are approved of by everyone: when you learn to walk and when you learn to read.'

– Penelope Fitzgerald

Introduction

An open door is a beautiful and welcoming image; it invites us in and leads us to a place beyond. A book has often been compared to a door – it's even shaped like one. And the poems in this Open Door collection will invite you in and lead you on, I hope, to many different and interesting worlds.

The Czech writer Miroslav Holub's poem called 'The Door' is a good place to start.

THE DOOR
Miroslav Holub

Go and open the door.
  Maybe outside there's
  a tree, or a wood,
  a garden,
  or a magic city.

Go and open the door.
  Maybe a dog's rummaging.
  Maybe you'll see a face,
or an eye,
or the picture
        of a picture.

Go and open the door.
  If there's a fog
  It will clear.

Go and open the door.
  Even if there's only
  the darkness ticking,
  even if there's only

the hollow wind,
    even if
        nothing
            is there,
go and open the door.

At least
there'll be
a draught.

Here, even in translation (by Ian Milner), we are reminded of the mystery and strangeness associated with an open door. We are also reminded that the ordinary and the wonderful, the familiar and the different, can be experienced once that door is opened. You may not always be at ease when you cross the threshold for the first time. You may find yourself wondering about the world you are now discovering. But you will be in a different place and 'At least there'll be a draught'.

Poetry is different from all other kinds of writing. It looks different on the page. It sounds different in the way that it connects in a very powerful, one-to-one relationship with the reader. Reading a poem is special and private. When we read a poem we know that we are not alone. Someone is speaking directly to us about something important to them – their thoughts and feelings, their way of looking at and understanding the world.

Some poems take us by the hand, others offer signposts. Some poems challenge, some poems amuse. And every poem tells us something not only about the poet but also about ourselves. The fifty or so poems in this collection offer a wide range of voices – old and young, male and female, from long ago and from our own time.

It doesn't take very long to read a poem but a poet's way of saying and a poet's way of seeing can stay with us for years. I hope you enjoy what these poems have to say and the way that they say it.

Niall MacMonagle

Here's a poem with a powerful plot, a mini-drama in eighty lines. The rhythm or movement builds up to create vivid scenes in the reader's mind. The complicated world of passion and betrayal is captured here in description and dialogue. Though Frankie was the one who was wronged to begin with, she is the one who ends up losing everything. The poet tells us that 'the story has no moral' but it still leaves you feeling 'That's just too bad.'

FRANKIE AND JOHNNY
Anonymous

Frankie and Johnny were lovers.
O my Gawd how they did love!
They swore to be true to each other;
As true as the stars above.
He was her man but he done her wrong.

Frankie went down to the hock-shop,
Went for a bucket of beer,
Said: 'O Mr Bartender
Has my loving Johnny been here?
He is my man but he's doing me wrong.'

'I don't want to make you no trouble,
I don't want to tell you no lie,
But I saw Johnny an hour ago
With a girl named Nelly Bly,
He is your man but he's doing you wrong.'

Frankie went down to the hotel,
She didn't go there for fun,
'Cause underneath her kimona

She toted a 44 Gun.
He was her man but he done her wrong.

Frankie went down to the hotel.
She rang the front-door bell,
Said: 'Stand back all you chippies
Or I'll blow you all to hell.
I want my man for he's doing me wrong.'

Frankie looked in through the key-hole
And there before her eye
She saw her Johnny on the sofa
A-loving up Nelly Bly.
He was her man; he was doing her wrong.

Frankie threw back her kimona,
Took out a big 44,
Root-a-toot-toot, three times she shot
Right through that hardware door.
He was her man but he was doing her wrong.

Johnny grabbed up his Stetson,
Said: 'O my Gawd Frankie don't shoot!'
But Frankie pulled hard on the trigger

And the gun went root-a-toot-toot.
She shot her man who was doing her wrong.

'Roll me over easy,
Roll me over slow,
Roll me over on my right side
'Cause my left side hurts me so.
I was her man but I done her wrong.'

'Bring out your rubber-tired buggy,
Bring out your rubber-tired hack;
I'll take my Johnny to the graveyard
But I won't bring him back.
He was my man but he done me wrong.

'Lock me in that dungeon,
Lock me in that cell,
Lock me where the north-east wind
Blows from the corner of Hell.
I shot my man 'cause he done me wrong.'

It was not murder in the first degree,
It was not murder in the third.
A woman simply shot her man

As a hunter drops a bird.
She shot her man 'cause he done her wrong.

Frankie said to the Sheriff,
'What do you think they'll do?'
The Sheriff said to Frankie,
'It's the electric-chair for you.
You shot your man 'cause he done you
    wrong.'

Frankie sat in the jail-house,
Had no electric fan.
Told her sweet little sister:
'There ain't no good in a man.
I had a man but he done me wrong.'

Once more I saw Frankie,
She was sitting in the Chair
Waiting for to go and meet her God
With the sweat dripping out of her hair.
He was a man but he done her wrong.

This story has no moral,
This story has no end,

This story only goes to show
That there ain't no good in men.
He was her man but he done her wrong.

This little poem was written by a schoolboy from the North of Ireland some years back. It won first prize in a poetry competition judged by Paul Muldoon. It seems so simple and yet it's fresh and inventive in the way it brings language alive. Professor Muldoon now teaches at Princeton University in the United States. Every year he asks his creative writing class to describe something in one line and in a way that makes you look at the world in a new way. That, according to Muldoon, is what the schoolboy did when he wrote about the tortoise going m-o-v-e-y, m-o-v-e-y. This poem is best read aloud and very slowly.

THE TORTOISE
Anonymous

The tortoise goes movey, movey.

'Western Wind' is almost five hundred years old but the feeling of longing and loneliness is a feeling someone experiences somewhere every day. The weather is wet and windy. The speaker imagines that he/she is with his/her lover in bed, safe and loving and warm and out of the wind and the rain's way.

WESTERN WIND
Anonymous

Western wind when will thou blow
The small rain down can rain –
Christ, if my love were in my arms
And I in my bed again!

[The original poem dates from 1520 and it's
interesting to see what English looked like then:

Westron wynde when wyll thow blow
The smalle rayne downe can rayne –
Cryst, yf my love wer in my armys
And I in my bed agayne!]

No one has had a trouble-free life when it comes to relationships. How could we be expected to like everyone? Or for everyone else to like us? 'If you don't like me just leave me alone' is all very well but sometimes we just get dug in. We pull and tear. We allow our interaction with other people to get the better of us. We poison things. William Blake speaks of how things go seriously wrong if we allow them to get worse and worse. In his poem, published in 1794, the enemy is destroyed but so too is the speaker. William Blake was born in London in 1757 where he lived poor and died poor. He was buried in an unmarked grave in London's Bunhill Fields public cemetery in 1827.

A POISON TREE
William Blake

I was angry with my friend:
I told my wrath, my wrath did end.
I was angry with my foe:
I told it not, my wrath did grow.

And I watered it in fears,
Night & morning with my tears:
And I sunned it with my smiles,
And with soft deceitful wiles.

And it grew both day and night,
Till it bore an apple bright.
And my foe beheld it shine,
And he knew that it was mine.

And into my garden stole,
And when the night had veiled the pole;
In the morning glad I see,
My foe outstretched beneath the tree.

Different artists all over the world have been drawn to the image of mother and child. It is one of the deepest bonds there is. A mother caring for her child and gathering up her child in her arms is a warm expression of love in this poem by Eavan Boland. Without mother and child life could not go on. The setting here is a late summer's evening in Dundrum, in the Dublin suburbs. It could be anywhere and always. Surrounding the central image of mother and child are beautiful images of safety (the house with its butter-yellow window) and riches and mystery (stars, moths, sweet apples). Eavan Boland was born in Dublin in 1944 and grew up in London and New York. She now teaches at Stanford University in California but her home is in Dundrum.

THIS MOMENT
Eavan Boland

A neighbourhood.
At dusk.

Things are getting ready
to happen
out of sight.

Stars and moths.
And rinds slanting around fruit.

But not yet.

One tree is black.
One window is yellow as butter.

A woman leans down to catch a child
who has run into her arms
this moment.

Stars rise.
Moths flutter.
Apples sweeten in the dark.

How should we live our lives? How do we want to live our lives? Whose life turns out the way we want? Which of us can predict the journey we travel? Lucy Brennan's life certainly didn't turn out the way it was supposed to but her poem still has a wonderful sense of achievement and contentment. Lucy Brennan was born in Dublin in 1931. She grew up in Cork and emigrated to Canada in 1957 where she now lives.

WHEN ALL IS SAID AND DONE
Lucy Brennan

what I wanted
was

to marry young

have children
and more children

dance and act up a storm

have a husband's love
that would never end

die last of my family

how was I to know
I would be my own woman at last

without all that

We all know the tune and we sing it once a year, the world over, at New Year. Some of us never know all the words of a song written in 1788. Here it is – Robbie Burns's world-famous poem that celebrates friendship, happy memories and hopes for the future. It's in Scots and several of the words are strange but an easier-to-read version follows the original. Robbie Burns, the son of a poor farmer, was born in Alloway, Scotland in 1759. His birthday, on 25 January, is celebrated world-wide with a Burns Supper. He died in 1796.

AULD LANG SYNE
Robert Burns

Should auld acquaintance be forgot,
And never brought to mind?
Should auld acquaintance be forgot,
And days of lang syne?

Chorus [repeated after every verse]

For auld lang syne, my dear,
For auld lang syne,
We'll take a cup of kindness yet
For auld lang syne.

We twa have run about the braes,
And pu'd the gowans fine,
But we've wandered mony a weary foot,
Sin' auld lang syne.

We twa hae paidled i' the burn,
From morning sun till dine;
But seas between us braid hae roared,
Sin' auld lang syne.

And there's a hand, my trusty fiere,
And give a hand o' thine;
And we'll tak a right gude willie waught,
For auld lang syne.

And surely ye'll be your pint-stowp,
And surely I'll be mine,
And we'll tak a cup o' kindness yet,
For auld lang syne.

[*'Auld Lang Syne'* means *'Long Ago'*; *'braes'*
means *'slopes'*; *'pu'd'* is *'pulled'*; *'gowans'* means
'daisies'; *'paidled'* is *'paddled'*; *'burn'* means
'stream'; *'dine'* means *'dinner'* (at noon); *'braid'*
is *'broad'*; *'fiere'* means *'friend'*; *'a right gude
willie waught'* is *'a really good long drink'*; *'be
your pint-stowp'* is *'pay for your pint cup'*.]

AULD LANG SYNE/LONG AGO

Should old acquaintance be forgot
And never brought to mind?
Should old acquaintance be forgot
And days of long ago?

For Long Ago my dear,
For Long Ago,
We'll drink a cup of kindness yet,
For Long Ago.

We two have run about the slopes
And pulled the daisies fine
But we've wandered many a weary foot
Since Long Ago.

We two have paddled in the stream
Since sunrise until noon
But broad seas between us have roared
Since Long Ago.

And there's a hand my trusty friend
And you give me your hand
And we'll take a really good long drink
For Long Ago.

And surely you'll pay for your pint cup
And I will pay for mine
And we'll drink a cup of kindness yet
For Long Ago.

Are people the same the world over? When Paddy Bushe travelled in Tibet everything he had heard about the people in that country was true. He came across the young smiling, welcoming Tibetan Shepherd boys, skilled at minding sheep on the dangerous slopes. But he also saw a savagery and no-reason-for-it violence in those same boys. Everything is wonderful until that vicious last line that stops you in your tracks. Paddy Bushe was born in Dublin in 1948. He now lives in Waterville, County Kerry near the spot where, according to legend, the first Celtic invaders landed in Ireland.

TIBETAN SHEPHERD BOYS
Paddy Bushe

It was all true, everything you'd read,
The open faces, the wide-eyed delight
In stroking the hairs of my arms,
The infectious, endless laughing.

It was wonderful, too, the agility
As they raced away after sheep,
Waving from high, dizzy paths,
Their good-byes bouncing between cliffs.

And I could see, from a distance,
The incredible speed and grace they showed
As they cut out and caught a wild goat
And kicked and stoned him, just for the hell of it.

Many of us have been on a Mediterranean holiday. Don Byrne in this poem catches the warm, easy, end-of-the-day feeling. It has been a day of boiling heat. But in early evening, after a shower, the body relaxes, is at ease with itself in the outside sitting room. It's both a people-watching poem and a vivid description of the body's sensation of itself as the sun goes down. Byrne makes words work here in an unusual way. For example, instead of saying Antonio and Kimon are smoking he makes it more interesting – 'Antonio cigarettes the breeze'. A wonderful and memorable holiday snapshot. Don Byrne was born in Ardara, County Donegal in 1955. He teaches maths in Dungloe and runs the family bicycle business in Ardara.

Ouzo Time
Don Byrne

Our day boils down to this:
brown hills still lit with sun,
the evening shadow's gift
of sitting room outside.

Our shower prints evaporate
before we towel dry
and scent the air
with aftersun.

Two German girls potato-peel,
chickens lance the fallen skins,
a rabbit soft-pads stony ground
and Sylvie's lost within *Le Monde.*

Antonio cigarettes the breeze
with Kimon. They relax within
a waterfall of easy Greek.
I roll the ouzo on my tongue.

Goat bells tinkle down the hill.
A waterpump beats from below,
its dark transfusion creeps along
cracked earth to vine, tomato.

Byron's poem, written in 1817, admits with a sweet sadness that life brings changes with it. As we grow older we change our ways. No one is forever young. Sometimes, however, we would like to be as we were. We would still like to go roving late into the night. But Byron reminds us that there comes a time when we leave that behind. The moon is still bright and beautiful. The night was made for loving and there are always younger people who will continue to rove under its light in search of romance and adventure. Lord Byron, of whom it was said that he was 'mad, bad and dangerous to know', was born in London in 1788. He fought with the Greeks against the Turks. He died of marsh fever at Missolonghi and was buried in Nottingham, England.

So We'll Go No More A-Roving

George Gordon, Lord Byron

I

So we'll go no more a-roving
    So late unto the night,
Though the heart be still as loving,
    And the moon be still as bright.

II

For the sword outwears its sheath,
    And the soul wears out the breast,
And the heart must pause to breathe,
    And Love itself have rest.

III

Though the night was made for loving,
    And the day returns too soon,
Yet we'll go no more a-roving
    By the light of the moon.

Sometimes only a moment is captured in a poem but that moment lives again and again, everytime that poem is read. In this poem by the Greek poet Constantine P. Cavafy a simple, ordinary moment is described. Though great wealth is mentioned, what emerges as even more important is youthful beauty. That we are told by the poet how the mirror feels makes it even more unusual. Cavafy was born in Alexandria, Egypt, of a Greek family. He worked as a civil servant and published very few poems during his lifetime. He died in 1933. The poem printed here is a translation by Rae Dalven.

THE MIRROR IN THE HALL
C.P. Cavafy

The wealthy home had in its entrance
an enormous, extremely old mirror,
that must have been bought at least eighty years ago.

An unusually handsome lad, a tailor's employee
(on Sundays an amateur athlete),
stood holding a parcel. He delivered it
to someone in the house, who carried it inside
to fetch the receipt. The tailor's employee
was left by himself, and he waited.
He approached the mirror and took a look at himself,
And he straightened his tie. Five minutes later
they brought back the receipt. He took it and left.

But the old mirror that had seen and seen,
During the long, long years of its existence,
thousands of objects and faces;
but this time the old mirror was delighted,
and it felt proud that it had received unto itself
for a few moments an image of flawless beauty.

At the turn of this millennium there are over six billion people living on planet Earth. Millions have lived and died down through the years. The dead live on in memory and thinking of them as watchful presences is a comforting idea. In Billy Collins's poem he creates a beautifully calming picture of heaven and of those who have gone before. He also gently reminds us that one day we will join them. Billy Collins was born in New York city in 1941. He was Poet Laureate of the United States and Professor of English at Lehman College, New York.

THE DEAD
Billy Collins

The dead are always looking down on us, they
 say,
while we are putting on our shoes or making a
 sandwich,
they are looking down through the glass-
 bottom boats of heaven
as they row themselves slowly through eternity.

They watch the tops of our heads moving
 below on earth,
and when we lie down in a field or on a couch,
 drugged perhaps by the hum of a warm
 afternoon,
they think we are looking back at them,

which makes them lift their oars and fall silent
and wait, like parents, for us to close our eyes.

Here is a poem that has a 'long ago' feeling to it. Yet the feeling within the poem is known to everyone in every age. We all want to find a place we can call home. Wherever it is, that place is special and important to us. The feeling of longing in the opening line is a feeling known to people everywhere who have been abandoned, forgotten, dispossessed or refugees. Padraic Colum was born in 1881 in County Longford and from 1914 lived in New York. He died in 1972.

AN OLD WOMAN OF THE ROADS
Padraic Colum

O, to have a little house!
To own the hearth and stool and all!
The heaped up sods upon the fire
The pile of turf again' the wall!

To have a clock with weights and chains,
And pendulum swinging up and down!
A dresser filled with shining delph,
Speckled and white and blue and brown!

I could be busy all the day
Clearing and sweeping hearth and floor,
And fixing on their shelf again
My white and blue and speckled store!

I could be quiet there at night
Beside the fire and by myself,
Sure of a bed, and loth to leave
The ticking clock and shining delph!

Och! But I'm weary of mist and dark,
And roads where there's never a house nor bush,
And tired I am of bog and road,
And the crying wind and the lonesome hush!

And I am praying to God on high,
And I am praying Him night and day,
For a little house – a house of my own –
Out of the wind's and the rain's way.

Poets spend more time alone than most, thinking, imagining, talking to themselves. In this short poem Pádraig J. Daly watches an everyday scene. A woman takes in the washing. A storm is on the way. What makes it special is how Daly thinks about these things. The washing is taken down off the sky, not down from the line, and he wonders if people still see God's presence in the natural world. Pádraig J. Daly was born in Dungarvan, County Waterford in 1943. He studied at UCD and in Rome and is now an Augustinian friar based in Wexford.

ON THE ROOFTOPS: ROME 1970
Pádraig J. Daly

We wait for the storm to break.
Signora Morandini has taken her washing
Down off the sky. The swallows annoy her.
God rides out on thunderclouds.
People come to office windows –
Perhaps to see him passing in the rain.

The world is a noisy place and getting noisier by the year. Whether it's true or not, we all think we are living busier lives. Do we ever take time out? Do we ever just stop and stare and do nothing? Doing nothing is very good for us at times. If we could just be idle for a few moments every day we'd be all the better for it. William Henry Davies was born in Wales. He tramped around America and Canada for six years and had to have a leg amputated after jumping from a moving train. He married in London and settled in the Cotswolds. He died in 1940.

LEISURE
W. H. Davies

What is this life if, full of care,
We have no time to stop and stare? –

No time to stand beneath the boughs
And stare as long as sheep or cows:

No time to see, when woods we pass,
Where squirrels hide their nuts in grass:

No time to see, in broad daylight,
Streams full of stars, like skies at night:

No time to turn at Beauty's glance,
And watch her feet, how they can dance:

No time to wait till her mouth can
Enrich that smile her eyes began?

A poor life this if, full of care,
We have no time to stand and stare.

Poetry is one way of storing the past. When people die they live on in our memories. We think about them not being here as we go on with our everyday lives. The past and the present connect.

In this poem Greg Delanty writes about his father-in-law a year after his death. Nature is reminding us always that life does and must go on, that we live on in nature and in memory. Greg Delanty was born in Cork in 1958. He now lives and works in Burlington, Vermont.

THE PRESENT
Greg Delanty

Sparrows mostly, but chickadees,
cardinals, finches, wild canaries
feed all day on our bird-house stairs.
Sunflower seeds, beautiful black tears
your father gave us only a year ago.
He is dead now. How were we to know?
Snow is a white sheet laid silently upon
the body of the earth. How the dead live on.

When Emily Dickinson died in 1886 she was unknown. Now she is one of the most famous poets in the world. She wrote 1,775 poems in all. Only a handful were published anonymously during her lifetime. Though all of them were short, each one contained powerful thoughts and feelings. In this poem she reminds us, in the image of a bird, that hope is something we all value. It never dies. No matter how bad things get we always hope for better times. Hope keeps us going and keeps us warm. Emily Dickinson was born in Amherst, Massachusetts, in 1830 and died there in 1886.

'"HOPE" IS THE THING WITH FEATHERS'
Emily Dickinson

'Hope' is the thing with feathers –
That perches in the soul –
And sings the tune without the words –
And never stops – at all –

And sweetest – in the Gale – is heard –
And sore must be the storm –
That could abash the little Bird
That kept so many warm –

I've heard it in the chillest land –
And on the strangest Sea –
Yet, never, in Extremity,
It asked a crumb of Me.

It is almost impossible to tell people how we feel about them face-to-face. Yet we are capable of very deep thoughts and feelings towards one another. In this father-and-son poem, Noel Duffy is remembering the easy awkwardness of Sunday walks with his father, who offers him a glimpse into the past and a link with a world that is disappearing. Neither the poet nor his father knew their grandfathers. Only photograph or story remain. Noel Duffy was born in Dublin in 1971. He studied physics at Trinity College and now lives in Galway where he teaches creative writing.

DAISY-CHAIN
Noel Duffy

Sometimes on Sundays we'd take
the old canal bank walk
from Broombridge to the Ashtown Cross,
my father picking daisies as we went

between questions of *How is school?*
and *Did you score any goals this week?*
my embarrassment at his interest
saying, *Fine* or *Only one this time.*

Often he would talk about the past,
of how his grandfather passed this spot

every day for nearly thirty years
as he drove the train from Castlebar

to Connolly Station, the canal water
his sign that he was nearly home,
until his early death in a red-brick
terraced house near Great Western Square,

my father saying, *I only knew him*
by a photograph the way you know my father
through me, as an image and likeness,
as a man about whom stories gather;

and all the while his fingers working
the stems, binding them together one
by one, a chain of flowers forming
in his hands until joining first to last

the circle was complete and he'd
give it to me to throw into the canal waters.
And forgetting school and football,
we'd watch it floating on the surface,

bobbing slightly in our world of lost
connections, the frail wreath pulled
slowly downstream by the current, towards
the steady, distant thunder of the lock.

Paul Durcan's way of looking at the world is fresh, funny and different. He often writes about everyday things, ordinary people. Government Buildings in any capital city are impressive and important places. But in this poem Durcan is not thinking about our Taoiseach and TDs gathered around the cabinet table for important meetings. Real people take over the poem and have a bit of fun. This poem will make you laugh and you'll never think about that cabinet table in the same way again. Paul Durcan was born in Dublin in 1944 and is one of Ireland's most popular poets. He lives in Ringsend, Dublin.

THE CABINET TABLE
Paul Durcan

Alice Gunn is a cleaner woman
Down at Government Buildings,
And after seven o'clock Mass last night
(Isn't it a treat to be able to go to Sunday Mass
On a Saturday! To sit down to Saturday Night TV
Knowing you've fulfilled your Sunday obligation!)
She came back over to The Flats for a cup of tea
(I offered her sherry but she declined –
Oh, I never touch sherry on a Saturday night –
Whatever she meant by that, I don't know).
She had us all in stitches, telling us
How one afternoon after a Cabinet Meeting
She got one of the security men
To lie down on the Cabinet Table,
And what she didn't do to him –
And what she did do to him –
She didn't half tell us;
But she told us enough to be going on with.
'Do you know what it is?' she says to me:
'No,' says I, 'what is it?'
'It's mahogany,' she says, 'pure mahogany.'

The birth of Christ was momentous and changed the course of human history. U. A. Fanthorpe writes about this earth-changing event in a matter-of-fact way. But in the closing lines there is an extraordinary sense of the importance of Christ's coming and the eternal life for those who follow Christ's teachings. Ursula Askham Fanthorpe was born in Kent in 1929 and became, in her own words, a 'middle-aged dropout'. She lives in Gloucestershire.

BC : AD
U. A. Fanthorpe

This was the moment when Before
Turned into After, and the future's
Uninvented timekeepers presented arms.

This was the moment when nothing
Happened. Only dull peace
Sprawled boringly over the earth.

This was the moment when even energetic Romans
Could find nothing better to do
Than counting heads in remote provinces.

And this was the moment
When a few farm workers and three
Members of an obscure Persian sect

Walked haphazard by starlight straight
Into the kingdom of heaven.

We talk about the weather more often than any other topic. Our moods often depend on what's happening overhead. Blue skies bring a very different day to driving, cold, persistent rain. In this poem Thomas Hardy is in a light-hearted mood in stanza one as he identifies with spring and summer. In the second stanza the weather is harsh and unfriendly and best avoided. Thomas Hardy was born in 1840 in Dorset. He wrote fifteen novels and almost a thousand poems. He died, aged eighty-seven, in 1928.

WEATHERS
Thomas Hardy

I

This is the weather the cuckoo likes,
    And so do I;
When showers betumble the chestnut spikes,
    And nestlings fly;
And the little brown nightingale bills his best,
And they sit outside at 'The Travellers' Rest',
And maids come forth sprig-muslin drest,
And citizens dream of the south and west,
    And so do I.

II

This is the weather the shepherd shuns,
    And so do I;
When beeches drip in browns and duns,
    And thresh, and ply;
And hill-hid tides throb, throe on throe,
And meadow rivulets overflow,
And drops on gate-bars hang in a row,
And rooks in families homeward go,
    And so do I.

The words Mid-Term Break spell magic in the minds of every schoolgirl and boy. But in this poem the mid-term break is totally unexpected and the feelings associated with it are ones of great pain and sorrow. The young boy must go home to heartbroken parents and the unbearable sadness of seeing his little four-year-old brother dead. Seamus Heaney was born in 1939 on a farm in County Derry. He was awarded the Nobel Prize for Literature in 1995 and has lived in Dublin since the 1970s.

MID-TERM BREAK
Seamus Heaney

I sat all morning in the college sick bay
Counting bells knelling classes to a close.
At two o'clock our neighbours drove me home.

In the porch I met my father crying –
He had always taken funerals in his stride –
And Big Jim Evans saying it was a hard blow.

The baby cooed and laughed and rocked the pram
When I came in, and I was embarrassed
By old men standing up to shake my hand

And tell me they were 'sorry for my trouble'.
Whispers informed strangers I was the eldest,
Away at school, as my mother held my hand

In hers and coughed out angry tearless sighs.
At ten o'clock the ambulance arrived
With the corpse, stanched and bandaged by the nurses.

Next morning I went up into the room. Snowdrops
And candles soothed the bedside; I saw him
For the first time in six weeks. Paler now,

Wearing a poppy bruise on his left temple,
He lay in the four-foot box as in his cot.
No gaudy scars, the bumper knocked him clear.

A four-foot box, a foot for every year.

Young men have gone to war down the centuries for different reasons. The young who die in battle have sacrificed their most precious possession – their young lives and the future that they will never live to see. In this poem the young men fought for their country because they did not want to disgrace it by acting cowardly. Housman imagines how the dead must feel and he gives them a voice. Alfred Edward Housman was born in Worcestershire in 1859. He was a Professor of Latin at Cambridge University and died in 1936. The poem does not have a title – just the number thirty-six in Roman numerals in a sequence of poems called More Poems.

XXXVI

A. E. Housman

Here dead lie we because we did not choose
  To live and shame the land from which we sprung.
Life, to be sure, is nothing much to lose;
  But young men think it is, and we were young.

Here is a snapshot of a lonely life but a quirky humour saves the poem from total misery. It's a celebration of eccentricity, of doing your own thing. And it reminds us of the most important lesson of all: that, in the end, we have to learn to live with ourselves. Pat Ingoldsby was born in Dublin and lives there still. He has said that if any of his poems 'ever surface in school or college textbooks when I'm dead and gone, I'll come back and haunt whoever's responsible'.

MORE OF ME
Pat Ingoldsby

I eat Jaffa Cakes in bed
at four o'clock in the morning
when I am lonely.

I eat lots of them
and they make my stomach fat.

I like to think
that I am growing
some more of me
to keep myself company.

An artist was once asked, 'When did you start painting?' and the artist replied, 'When did you stop?' Children's minds are fresh and alive and their imaginations are not hemmed in by rules. In this poem anything goes and the boy's imagination creates a marvellous picture. He includes what is near and far, what is familiar and exotic. The result is a happy painting filled with colourful life. This poem won first place in the Arvon Foundation Poetry Prize 2004. Joe Kane was born in Dublin in 1952. He now works as a potter/ceramicist in Donegal.

THE BOY WHO NEARLY WON THE TEXACO ART COMPETITION
Joe Kane

for Ted Hughes

he took a large sheet
of white paper and on this
he made the world an african world
of flat topped trees and dried grasses
and he painted an elephant in the middle
and a lion with a big mane and several giraffes
stood over the elephant and some small animals to fill

in the gaps he worked all day had a bath this
    was saturday

on sunday he put six jackals
in the world and a great big snake
and buzzards in the sky and tickbirds
on the elephants back he drew down blue
from the sky to make a river and got the elephants
legs all wet and smudged and one of the jackals
    got drowned
he put red flowers in the front of the picture and
    daffodils in the bottom corners
and his dog major chewing a bone and mrs murphys
    two cats tom and jerry
and milo the milkman with a cigarette
    in the corner of his mouth
and his merville dairy float pulled by his wonder
    horse trigger
that would walk when he said click click
    and the holy family
in the top right corner with the donkey and cow
and sheep and baby jesus and got the 40A bus
on monday morning in to abbey street to hand
it in and the man on the door said
thats a sure winner

What was the world like long ago? And what will the world be like long after we've gone? We sometimes look back; sometimes, we try to imagine the future. Some things, though, have remained and, we like to think, will remain the same: birds and trees and the rain. As Patrick Kavanagh says in another poem ('Thank You, Thank You') – 'We are not alone in our loneliness;/ Others have been here and known/ Griefs we thought our special own.' Patrick Kavanagh was born in County Monaghan in 1904. He lived in London and settled in Dublin, where he died in 1967.

WET EVENING IN APRIL
Patrick Kavanagh

The birds sang in the wet trees
And as I listened to them it was a hundred years from now
And I was dead and someone else was listening to them.
But I was glad I had recorded for him the melancholy.

'The sun rises in spite of everything' says the poet Derek Mahon. A new day brings new possibilities, new opportunities. This poem by Brendan Kennelly has a spring in its step as it celebrates the everyday, the ordinary. It reminds us that the everyday is special, that the ordinary is extraordinary. Though set in the city, it shows us that nature's eternal presence is a life-force in our sometimes chaotic lives. Brendan Kennelly was born in Ballylongford, County Kerry in 1936. He recently retired as Professor of English at Trinity College, Dublin.

BEGIN
Brendan Kennelly

Begin again to the summoning birds
to the sight of light at the window,
begin to the roar of morning traffic
all along Pembroke Road.
Every beginning is a promise
born in light and dying in dark
determination and exaltation of springtime

flowering the way to work.
Begin to the pageant of queuing girls
the arrogant loneliness of swans in the canal
bridges linking the past and future
old friends passing though with us still.
Begin to the loneliness that cannot end
since it perhaps is what makes us begin,
begin to wonder at unknown faces
at crying birds in the sudden rain
at branches stark in the willing sunlight
at seagulls foraging for bread
at couples sharing a sunny secret
alone together while making good.
Though we live in a world that dreams of ending
that always seems about to give in
something that will not acknowledge conclusion
insists that we forever begin.

As the song says, 'Breaking up is hard to do'. In Nick Laird's poem everything becomes ordinary when he and his lover go their separate ways. The empty jeweller's window, all sparkle and glitter gone, is a familiar and effective image of the new emptiness they have to face. The frequent use of the full stop – in the opening two stanzas, every line is a sentence – indicates a slowing down, a sadness. Nick Laird was born in County Tyrone in 1975. He studied law at Cambridge University and is now a full-time writer. He lives in London.

DONE
Nick Laird

We've come to bag the evidence.
This might be the scene of a murder.
Dustsheets and silence and blame.

The flat empties its stomach into the hall.
We have given back letters and eaten our words.
You wrote off the Volvo. I gave you verrucas.

And like the window of a jeweller's after closing
the shelves in the study offer up nothing.
I slowly take the steps down one by one,

and for the first time maybe,
notice the chaos, the smouldering traffic,
the litter, bystanders, what have you

In Patrick Kavanagh's wonderful novel Tarry Flynn, *Tarry's mother says, 'Lord, but doesn't the years slip by in a hurry.' The passing of time has preoccupied all of us at some stage. When Philip Larkin sees the trees in early summer coming into leaf, he thinks not only of the future and warm, slow days but also has an underlying feeling of heartbreak. We live, we die, but, if the trees manage to disguise their growing old, then we too should make the most of our living and begin afresh, afresh, afresh. Philip Larkin was born in Coventry in 1922. He worked as a librarian in Belfast and Hull, where he spent over half of his life. He died in 1985.*

THE TREES
Philip Larkin

The trees are coming into leaf
Like something almost being said;
The recent buds relax and spread,
Their greenness is a kind of grief.

Is it that they are born again
And we grow old? No, they die too.
Their yearly trick of looking new
Is written down in rings of grain.

Yet still the unresting castles thresh
In fullgrown thickness every May.
Last year is dead, they seem to say,
Begin afresh, afresh, afresh.

We get over things eventually. Memories, once painful, give way, in time, to acceptance, a feeling of 'getting-on-with-life'. The speaker in Anne Le Marquand Hartigan's poem is now strong enough not to remember the pain that she once associated with the two white cups. Anne Hartigan was born in 1929 and has lived in Ireland since 1962. She now lives in Dublin.

Cup
Anne Le Marquand Hartigan

I no longer need to remember you
as I take out the two white cups
you gave me. Wide cups, from France.

Now I just look at a moon whiteness,
their silence. Waiting for the full
of rich roast coffee, the sugar, the cream.

I fill this emptiness. Savour the aroma
as I lift the cup to my lips.
And no longer taste any vinegar.

Sorrows can weigh us down, so much so that we can feel useless. And though we are unable to help we desperately want to. Joan McBreen here writes of a family she knows in a time of terrible stress and heartbreak. The grief is everywhere – in the blinding rain, the word 'climb', the abandoned bike, the hurtling train. Consolation is not possible. The poet, however, records the pain, an emotion we can identify with. Joan McBreen was born in Sligo in 1944 and she now lives in Tuam, County Galway.

PORTRAIT OF PARENTS AND CHILD
Joan McBreen

Sunday afternoon, I drive to my friend
in blinding rain. I climb the steps
to her kitchen door. The husband greets me,
their child does not look up from his game.

This boy no longer has eye-lashes or hair,
his face is pale, his mother's eyes
are vacant with grief,
her husband's eyes despair.

The child's bicycle is abandoned
in the yard; the dog slouches towards
the shed. We sit at the table,
tea is carefully poured. We talk.

Sun breaks through rain,
light enters the room. The cold sun
has travelled great distances of space,
is ignored by mother, father and child.

The spring blossoms in the mind
interweave with thoughts of pain.
This burning behind my eyes persists
and far away I hear

sounds of a train hurtling into the dark.

The relationship between parent and child is a deep and mysterious and never-ending relationship. Even death does not end it. We remember people even though they die and we can go on having conversations with them. Paula Meehan had a difficult relationship with her mother but it was a strong one. In this honest account the good and the bad times are captured. Fifteen years after her mother died Paula Meehan did go back to visit her grave. 'One day I got up and knew I was ready for it. I had made my peace with her spirit. It took that long to work out whatever her legacy was to me.' Paula Meehan was born in Dublin in 1955. She studied at Trinity College and now lives in North County Dublin.

THE PATTERN
Paula Meehan

Little has come down to me of hers,
a sewing machine, a wedding band,
a clutch of photos, the sting of her hand
across my face in one of our wars

when we had grown bitter and apart.
Some say that's the fate of the eldest daughter.
I wish now she'd lasted till after
I'd grown up. We might have made a new start

as women without tags like *mother, wife,*
sister, daughter, taken our chances from there.
At forty-two she headed for god knows where.
I've never gone back to visit her grave.

*

First she'd scrub the floor with Sunlight soap,
an armreach at a time. When her knees grew sore
she'd break for a cup of tea, then start again
at the door with lavender polish. The smell
would percolate back through the flat to us,
her brood banished to the bedroom.

And as she buffed the wax to a high shine
did she catch her own face coming clear?
Did she net a glimmer of her true self?
Did her mirror tell what mine tells me?
I have her shrug and go on
knowing history has brought her to her knees.

She'd call us in and let us skate around
in our socks. We'd grow solemn as planets
in an intricate orbit about her.

★

She's bending over crimson cloth,
the younger kids are long in bed.
Late summer, cold enough for a fire,
she works by fading light
to remake an old dress for me.
It's first day back at school tomorrow.

★

'Pure lambswool. Plenty of wear in it yet.
You know I wore this when I went out with your Da.
I was supposed to be down in a friend's house,
your Granda caught us at the corner.
He dragged me in by the hair – it was long as yours
    then –
in front of the whole street.

70

He called your Da every name under the sun,
cornerboy, lout; I needn't tell you
what he called me. He shoved my whole head
under the kitchen tap, took a scrubbing brush
and carbolic soap and in ice-cold water he scrubbed
every spick of lipstick and mascara off my face.
Christ but he was a right tyrant, your Granda.
It'll be over my dead body anyone harms a hair
    of your head.'

                    *

She must have stayed up half the night
to finish the dress. I found it airing at the fire,
three new copybooks on the table and a bright
bronze nib, St Christopher strung on a silver wire,

as if I were embarking on a perilous journey
to uncharted realms. I wore that dress
with little grace. To me it spelt poverty,
the stigma of the second hand. I grew enough to pass

it on by Christmas to the next in line. I was sizing
up the world beyond our flat patch by patch
daily after school, and fitting each surprising
city street to city square to diamond. I'd watch

the Liffey for hours pulsing to the sea

and the coming and going of ships,
certain that one day it would carry me
to Zanzibar, Bombay, the Land of the Ethiops.

*

There's a photo of her taken in the Phoenix Park
alone on a bench surrounded by roses
as if she had been born to formal gardens.
She stares out as if unaware
that any human hand held the camera, wrapped
entirely in her own shadow, the world beyond her
already a dream, already lost. She's
eight months pregnant. Her last child.

*

Her steel needles sparked and clacked,
the only other sound a settling coal
or her sporadic mutter
at a hard part in the pattern.
She favoured sensible shades:
Moss Green, Mustard, Beige.

I dreamt a robe of a colour
so pure it became a word.

Sometimes I'd have to kneel
an hour before her by the fire,

72

a skein around my outstretched hands,
while she rolled wool into balls.
If I swam like a kite too high
amongst the shadows on the ceiling
or flew like a fish in the pools
of pulsing light, she'd reel me firmly
home, she'd land me at her knees.

Tongues of flame in her dark eyes,
she'd say, 'One of these days I must
teach you to follow a pattern.'

Milosz was born in Lithuania and lived through times of great political unrest and uncertainty. He lived in California for many years and he wrote this poem there when he was sixty. In 'Gift' he's putting the past behind him and has managed to leave all the bad things there. The poem paints a beautiful picture of early morning in the Berkeley hills across the bay from San Francisco. Czeslaw Milosz (pronounced CHESS-wahf MEE-wash) was born in Szetejnie, Lithuania in 1911. He wrote in Polish and in English and died in 2004.

GIFT
Czeslaw Milosz

A day so happy.
Fog lifted early, I worked in the garden.
Hummingbirds were stopping over honeysuckle
    flowers.
There was no thing on earth I wanted to possess.
I knew no one worth my envying him.
Whatever evil I had suffered, I forgot.
To think that once I was the same man did not
    embarrass me.
In my body I felt no pain.
When straightening up, I saw the blue sea and
    sails.

If a poem makes us smile, then sometimes that's more than enough. The first three lines of 'Celia Celia' are flat and ordinary and match the speaker's mood. And then there's a marvellous lift in the closing line when the speaker thinks his very own private thought and we find ourselves smiling. Adrian Mitchell was born in London in 1932.

CELIA CELIA
Adrian Mitchell

When I am sad and weary
When I think all hope has gone
When I walk along High Holborn
I think of you with nothing on.

Every person is a mystery and no other human being is totally knowable. Brownlee upped and left – no explanation, no apology, no excuse. But this poem leaves us wondering and imagining a life for Brownlee beyond the fields. Where did he go? And was he happier for having made that brave decision? Paul Muldoon was born in Portadown, County Armagh in 1951. He published his first book at twenty-one and is now a Professor of English at Princeton University.

WHY BROWNLEE LEFT
Paul Muldoon

Why Brownlee left, and where he went,
Is a mystery even now.
For if a man should have been content
It was him; two acres of barley,
One of potatoes, four bullocks,
A milker, a slated farmhouse.
He was last seen going out to plough
On a March morning, bright and early.

By noon Brownlee was famous;
They had found all abandoned, with
The last rig unbroken, his pair of black
Horses, like man and wife,
Shifting their weight from foot to
Foot, and gazing into the future.

In this father and son poem the actual car journey becomes an image for life's journey. The speaker is aware of his son's sense of wonder, the freshness with which he views everything. But the poem also explores how the journey we make, the road ahead, must ultimately be undertaken alone. The stars remind us of our fragile, tiny, precious lives. John O'Donnell was born in Dublin where he works as a barrister.

WATCHING STARS
John O'Donnell

for William

We cover miles together, you and I
Rolling over the roads. You are
Sleep-suited, strapped in your child's seat,
An astronaut before blast-off.
Ahead of us the evening waits
For stars to emerge, as we do,
Watching the slate-blue sky until you

Are pointing suddenly amazed
At the first new far-off gleam
That gazes back at you. How near we seem
As I try to explain their distance,
Afraid of light years that must pass
Between us, space opening endlessly
In front of you as we drive towards

Darkened towns: the shops all closed, the schools
Silent. The empty insistent streets.
But you are asleep and dreaming now,
A glimpse of curls in my rear-view mirror.
Some day I'll look back to find you
Grown up and tugging at the handle,
Anxious to be gone

Into the night. The road ahead. And always
The stars, glinting above us
Like children from another time.
They whisper:
> We have been here before memory and loss,
> Our light remembered love and pain.
> We see. And are watching still.

Dennis O'Driscoll's parents died when he was a teenager. He and his brothers and sisters had to carry that sorrow into the rest of their lives. 'I'm getting on fine' is easily and often said and this poem tries to make the best of a sad situation. But sometimes we wonder how things might have been. The final line is the voice of quiet heartbreak. Dennis O'Driscoll was born in Thurles in 1954, works as a civil servant in Dublin and lives in Naas, County Kildare.

YEARS AFTER
Dennis O'Driscoll

And yet we managed fine.

We missed your baking for a time.
And yet were we not better off
without cream-hearted sponge cakes,
flaky, rhubarb-oozing pies?

Linoleum-tiled rooms could no longer
presume on your thoroughgoing scrub;
and yet we made up for our neglect,
laid hardwood timber floors.

Windows shimmered less often.
And yet we got around to
elbow-greasing them eventually.
Your daily sheet-and-blanket

rituals of bedmaking were more
than we could hope to emulate.
And yet the duvets we bought
brought us gradually to sleep.

Declan and Eithne (eleven
and nine respectively at the time)
had to survive without your packed
banana sandwiches, wooden spoon

deterrent, hugs, multivitamins.
And yet they both grew strong:
you have unmet grandchildren,
in-laws you never knew.

Yes, we managed fine, made
breakfasts and made love,
took on jobs and mortgages,
set ourselves up for life.

And yet. And yet. And yet.

Some people we know will die before we do. That's just the way it is. Grace Paley's friend died but Paley imagined meeting her on a bus in New York city. The lines on the page are broken; it's as if she is trying to piece things together and two old friends, one dead, the other alive, have a conversation. The one who is alive had to get on with her life. And there's something very sad about her friend not knowing about all that has gone on since she died, even that she gets off at a different bus stop. Grace Paley was born in New York in 1922.

I SEE MY FRIEND EVERYWHERE
Grace Paley

First she died   then on the bus
I saw her   my old friend dropped
her half fare into the slot
looked up   her eyes humorous
intelligent   cap of white hair
shining   I asked her   how's the boy
these days   not so good but you
know that   your work   is it going
well?   what work she whispered   (bitterly
I thought)   are you all right?   why
do you ask?   I was afraid of her

the bus rocked and bumped over and
through New York   unsteady   I called out
STOP this is where I get off   here?
since when?   oh for the last couple
of years   she nearly touched my hand
yes   I said   you were still alive

Here is a wife and mother under attack from all sides. Her husband and children sum her up as if she were being examined. The poem is a catalogue of disappointment and failure until everything switches in the closing lines. Then she has the last word and earns an A grade for independence. Linda Pastan was born in 1932. She grew up in New York and lives in Washington, D.C.

MARKS
Linda Pastan

My husband gives me an A
for last night's supper,
an incomplete for my ironing,
a B plus in bed.
My son says I am average,
an average mother, but if
I put my mind to it
I could improve.
My daughter believes
in Pass/Fail and tells me
I pass. Wait 'til they learn
I'm dropping out.

As we pass through life we see many beautiful, natural things but they too do not last. Padraic Pearse speaks of how the world's beauty makes him sad. He speaks of how everything that is young must change, grow old and die. In this poem heaven is on earth – evening sunshine, an unspoilt natural world, innocent children at play. But that heaven does not last and the poem's final word is lonely on a line of its own. Padraic Pearse, an Irish patriot and activist, was born in 1879. He was executed by firing squad in Kilmainham Jail on 3 May 1916.

THE WAYFARER
Padraic Pearse

The beauty of the world hath made me sad,
This beauty that will pass;
Sometimes my heart hath shaken with great joy
To see a leaping squirrel in a tree,
Or a red lady-bird upon a stalk,
Or little rabbits in a field at evening,
Lit by a slanting sun,
Or some green hill where shadows drifted by
Some quiet hill where mountainy man hath sown
And soon would reap; near to the gate of Heaven;
Or children with bare feet upon the sands
Of some ebbed sea, or playing on the streets
Of little towns in Connacht,
Things young and happy.
And then my heart hath told me:
These will pass,
Will pass and change, will die and be no more,
Things bright and green, things young and happy;
And I have gone upon my way
Sorrowful.

How will we be remembered by those whom we knew and by those who knew us? When we lose a friend, someone we love, naturally we are sad. When we ourselves die we will be remembered just as we remember those who die before us. In this sonnet Christina Rossetti asks that she be remembered but if remembering only brings sorrow then she would prefer to be forgotten by those whom she knew and loved. She does not want to be the cause of their sadness. Christina Rossetti was born in 1830 and died in 1894. She wrote the poem 'Remember' in one day.

REMEMBER
Christina Rossetti

Remember me when I am gone away,
Gone far away into the silent land;
When you can no more hold me by the hand,
Nor I half turn to go, yet turning stay.
Remember me when no more day by day
You tell me of our future that you planned:
Only remember me; you understand
It will be late to counsel then or pray,
Yet if you should forget me for a while
And afterwards remember, do not grieve:
For if the darkness and corruption leave
A vestige of the thoughts that once I had,
Better by far you should forget and smile
Than that you should remember and be sad.

The words 'red roses' are often associated with love and affection. In Anne Sexton's unforgettable poem about domestic violence the red roses in the song become the bruises on the little boy's body. And yet, at the heart of the poem is the love Tommy has for his mother even though she abuses him. When she asks him to lie he does so because of the complicated nature of their love. Anne Sexton was born in Newton, Massachusetts in 1928. After the birth of her daughter Sexton suffered mental breakdowns. She began writing poetry in 1957 and was Professor of Creative Writing at Boston University. She committed suicide in 1974.

RED ROSES
Anne Sexton

Tommy is three and when he's bad
his mother dances with him.
She puts on the record,
'Red Roses for a Blue Lady'
and throws him across the room.

Mind you,
she never laid a hand on him,
only the wall laid a hand on him.
He gets red roses in different places,
the head, that time he was as sleepy as a river,
the back, that time he was a broken scarecrow,
the arm like a diamond had bitten it,
the leg, twisted like a licorice stick,
all the dance they did together,
Blue Lady and Tommy.
You fell, she said, just remember you fell.
I fell, is all he told the doctors
in the big hospital. A nice lady came
and asked him questions but because
he didn't want to be sent away he said, I fell.
He never said anything else although he could talk fine.
He never told about the music
or how she'd sing and shout
holding him up and throwing him.

He pretends he is her ball.
He tries to fold up and bounce
But he squashes like fruit.
For he loves Blue Lady and the spots
Of red red roses he gives her.

Shakepeare wrote 154 sonnets in all and it is not difficult to see why this is one of the best known. We all know life's ups and downs. One of the great comforts when we're down is knowing that there are people who will always believe in us and forgive us and accept us for what we are through the darker days. The poem is four hundred years old but it was true the day it was written and it is true now. Shakespeare was born in Stratford-Upon-Avon in 1564. He spent twenty years in London acting and writing his now world-famous plays and died in Stratford in 1616.

SONNET 29
William Shakespeare

When in disgrace with Fortune and men's eyes,
I all alone beweep my outcast state,
And trouble deaf heaven with my bootless cries,
And look upon myself and curse my fate,
Wishing me like to one more rich in hope,
Featured like him, like him with friends possessed,
Desiring this man's art, and that man's scope,
With what I most enjoy contented least;
Yet in these thoughts myself almost despising,
Haply I think on thee, and then my state,
Like to the lark at break of day arising
From sullen earth, sings hymns at heaven's gate;
For thy sweet love remembered such wealth brings,
That then I scorn to change my state with kings.

*In the ordinary scheme of things we grow up,
we grow old and we die. The death of a young
person seems to contradict and mock every-
thing that life ought to be. Eileen Sheehan, in
this poem, looks at her son in his troubled sleep
and feels helpless. But she imagines her son
lost in a dream in which he and his two dead
friends are back in the world before the car
crash. All three are free and easy, playing ball.
Eileen Sheehan was born in County Kerry
and she now lives in Killarney.*

WAKING
Eileen Sheehan

I tiptoe the width of the landing
to check on my eldest child.

The curtains hanging open
the room half bright with streetlight,

he is sprawled
like any teenager
suddenly too broad
for his narrow bed,

his eyes in shadow,
his jawline shadowed
like a man's.

I go no further
than the door

for here in this dim room
sleeps a grief too deep
for a mother's healing kiss.

Yet he smiles in his sleep:
tossing ball on the green
with his two dead friends.

Until that Sunday morning
when it all came
crashing in,

death was a too-big jumper
stored on the highest shelf.

I have watched him,
tentatively
easing it on;
daily growing into it.

Life is a series of hellos and goodbyes and though goodbyes are difficult we have to get used to them. And in the end we have to say goodbye to life. Everything and everyone we ever loved – well, we have to let them go. Henry Shukman remembers, as a boy, playing with the idea of goodbye, imitating television characters. Then he remembers Religion class when he thought of Christ on the cross and imagined how he would rather live a little longer, even when there was nothing to drink but vinegar, than give up on life.

Snowy Morning
Henry Shukman

When we were nine or ten and used to play
at dying – hands clasped to the chest,
Goodbye, beautiful world, I love you! –
we didn't believe it could ever really be done.

Say goodbye to *everything*? A gunshot wound
in 'Alias Smith and Jones' could set us thinking –
please please don't die – or a feathered mess
that had been a pigeon squashed on the road.

Even Divinity class, that final sponge of vinegar
on a speartip. Goodbye, beautiful vinegar.
Now under the shag of decades, after so much
contact with things, it takes a morning like this.

Snow has fallen, a light crust. On the white field
green trails zigzag where the horses wandered,
a crazy scribble shows where they fed.
There they are now, two statues stooping.

All the ewes are sitting, thawing their grass.
Puddles crunch like caramel. Little snowfalls
crumble down a hedge. The silver-birch
trembles in its own twigs' shadows.

And under the rusty chestnut I walk
through a rain of crystals. There isn't much to say.
This is the day that decides by itself to be beautiful.
This field is a bride. How are we to say goodbye?

The human race has lived on planet Earth for some time but we have yet to live together in harmony. We hate each other for foolish reasons: for how we look, what we believe, where we come from. Wole Soyinka writes out of his own experience and, though the phone with its push buttons is out of date, the distrust and racism, unfortunately, are not.

Wole Soyinka was born in Nigeria in 1934 and was awarded the Nobel Prize for Literature in 1986.

TELEPHONE CONVERSATION
Wole Soyinka

The price seemed reasonable, location
Indifferent. The landlady swore she lived
Off premises. Nothing remained
But self-confession. 'Madam,' I warned,
'I hate a wasted journey – I am African.'
Silence. Silenced transmissions of
Pressurized good-breeding. Voice, when it came,
Lipstick-coated, long gold-rolled
Cigarette-holder pipped. Caught I was, foully.

'HOW DARK?' . . . I had not misheard . . . 'ARE
     YOU LIGHT
OR VERY DARK?' Button B. Button A. Stench
Of rancid breath of public hide-and-speak.
Red booth. Red pillar-box. Red double-tiered
Omnibus squelching tar. It was real! Shamed
By ill-mannered silence, surrender
Pushed dumbfoundment to beg simplification.
Considerate she was, varying the emphasis –

'ARE YOU DARK? OR VERY LIGHT?'
     Revelation came.

'You mean – like plain or milk chocolate?'
Her assent was clinical, crushing in its light
Impersonality. Rapidly, wavelength adjusted,
I chose, 'West African sepia' – and as an
    afterthought,
'Down in my passport.' Silence for
    spectroscopic
Flight of fancy, till truthfulness clanged her
    accent
Hard on the mouthpiece 'WHAT'S THAT?',
    conceding.
'DON'T KNOW WHAT THAT IS.' 'Like
    brunette.'

THAT'S DARK, ISN'T IT?' 'Not
    altogether.'
'Facially, I am brunette, but madam, you
    should see
'The rest of me. Palm of my hand, soles of
    my feet
'Are a peroxide blonde. Friction, caused –
'Foolishly, madam – by sitting down, has
    turned
'My bottom raven black – One moment
    madam!' – sensing

Her receiver rearing on the thunder-clap
About my ears – 'Madam,' I pleaded,
   'wouldn't you rather
'See for yourself?'

Though lonely, lonely, lonely, it is easy to see why this little poem is not only a key twentieth-century poem but also a favourite among poetry lovers. The powerful image of the drowning figure becomes a haunting symbol of our need to communicate. Thousands live lonely lives and our need for friendship and love is not always recognised or understood. Stevie Smith, whose real name was Florence Margaret Smith, was born in Hull in 1902. Her father abandoned the family and Stevie moved to London when she was four with her mother and sister to live with an aunt at 1 Avondale Road, Palmers Green. Stevie, never marrying, lived there for the rest of her life.

Not Waving but Drowning
Stevie Smith

Nobody heard him, the dead man,
But still he lay moaning:
I was much further out than you thought
And not waving but drowning.

Poor chap, he always loved larking
And now he's dead
It must have been too cold for him his heart
  gave way,
They said.

Oh, no no no, it was too cold always
(Still the dead one lay moaning)
I was much too far out all my life
And not waving but drowning.

This poem, first published in 1851, paints a very clear picture of a majestic bird in a dramatic landscape. We are high above the sea where this magnificent eagle bird reigns and all about is the great blue emptiness. Everything is still and quiet in the first stanza. In the second stanza Tennyson creates a brilliant sense of how high the mountains are from where the eagle watches. The sea way down below is crawling; the eagle is eagle eyed. And then the powerful energy of the bird as it swoops. Tennyson, Queen Victoria's favourite poet, was born in 1809 and died in 1892.

THE EAGLE
Alfred, Lord Tennyson

He clasps the crag with crooked hands;
Close to the sun in lonely lands,
Ringed with the azure world, he stands.

The wrinkled sea beneath him crawls:
He watches from his mountain walls,
And like a thunderbolt he falls.

Here is a poem in which nothing and every-thing happens. Memory holds the very ordinary, uneventful moment and it becomes special. The June afternoon is captured through eye and ear. Though the poem begins in the stuffy, confined space of a railway carriage, it ends with a picture of beautiful countryside that stretches for miles and endless birdsong. Edward Thomas was born in 1878, fell in love at sixteen with an eighteen-year-old and married her. When he was thirty-seven he enlisted in the army and was killed during the First World War on Easter Monday, 1917.

ADLESTROP
Edward Thomas

Yes. I remember Adlestrop –
The name, because one afternoon
Of heat the express-train drew up there
Unwontedly. It was late June.

The steam hissed. Someone cleared his throat.
No one left and no one came
On the bare platform. What I saw
Was Adlestrop – only the name

And willows, willow-herb, and grass,
And meadowsweet, and haycocks dry,
No whit less still and lonely fair
Than the high cloudlets in the sky.

And for that minute a blackbird sang
Close by, and round him, mistier,
Farther and farther, all the birds
Of Oxfordshire and Gloucestershire.

Memory makes us what we are. In this poem by Wordsworth he is reminding us of its magical and amazing power. We can re-live the past and re-visit special moments. And by doing so we can re-create, as Wordsworth does here, a wonderful happiness. This world-famous poem is usually known as 'The Daffodils', though Wordsworth never gave it that title. And even though it is about daffodils, ten thousand of them, it is more about remembering. William Wordsworth was born in 1770 in the Lake District. He was orphaned in his early teens and looked on Nature as his foster parent. He died in 1850.

I WANDERED LONELY AS A CLOUD
William Wordsworth

I wandered lonely as a cloud
That floats on high o'er vales and hills,
When all at once I saw a crowd,
A host of golden daffodils;
Beside the lake, beneath the trees,
Fluttering and dancing in the breeze.

Continuous as the stars that shine
And twinkle on the milky way,
They stretched in never-ending line
Along the margin of a bay:
Ten thousand saw I at a glance,
Tossing their heads in sprightly dance.

The waves beside them danced; but they
Out-did the sparkling waves in glee:
A poet could not but be gay,
In such a jocund company:
I gazed – and gazed – but little thought
What wealth the show to me had brought:

For oft, when on my couch I lie
In vacant or in pensive mood,
They flash upon that inward eye
Which is the bliss of solitude;
And then my heart with pleasure fills,
And dances with the daffodils.

This poem begins with traffic and concrete and busyness. But the horses bring the poet and reader to a much more beautiful world of twilight and shadows and kindness. The modern world is forgotten as the timeless world of horses at ease in a field takes over. Such moments are rare but enriching and they help us on our way on life's road. James Wright was born in 1927 in Ohio and died in 1980.

A BLESSING
James Wright

Just off the highway to Rochester, Minnesota,
Twilight bounds softly forth on the grass.
And the eyes of those two Indian ponies
Darken with kindness.
They have come gladly out of the willows
To welcome my friend and me.
We step over the barbed wire into the pasture
Where they have been grazing all day, alone.
They ripple tensely, they can hardly contain their
  happiness
That we have come.

They bow shyly as wet swans. They love each other.
There is no loneliness like theirs.
At home once more,
They begin munching the young tufts of spring in
    the darkness.
I would like to hold the slenderer one in my arms,
For she has walked over to me
And nuzzled my left hand.
She is black and white,
Her mane falls wild on her forehead,
And the light breeze moves me to caress her long ear
That is delicate as the skin over a girl's wrist.
Suddenly I realise
That if I stepped out of my body I would break
Into blossom.

Everyone knows the feeling, some time or other, of wanting to get away from it all. When Yeats was a young man he was walking down a London street and the tinkling sound of water in a little toy fountain in a shop window reminded him of Sligo and the very happy times he spent there. In this, his most famous poem, he dreams of being on an island in Lough Gill, County Sligo, and finding peace and happiness there. In 2000 The Irish Times *asked its readers, 'What is your favourite Irish poem?' Over 3,500 people replied and Yeats's 'The Lake Isle of Innisfree' was the most popular one. William Butler Yeats was born in Dublin in 1865. He spent two-thirds of his life outside Ireland, was awarded the Nobel Prize for Literature in 1923 and died in France in 1939. He is buried in Drumcliff churchyard in County Sligo.*

The Lake Isle of Innisfree
W. B. Yeats

I will arise and go now and go to Innisfree,
And a small cabin build there of clay and
    wattles made;
Nine bean-rows will I have there, a hive for
    the honey-bee,
And live alone in the bee-loud glade.

And I shall have some peace there, for peace
    comes dropping slow,
Dropping from the veils of the morning to
    where the cricket sings;
There midnight's all a glimmer, and noon a
    purple glow,
And evening full of the linnet's wings.

I will arise and go now, for always night and
    day
I hear lake water lapping with low sounds by
    the shore;
While I stand on the roadway, or on the
    pavements grey,
I hear it in the deep heart's core.

ACKNOWLEDGMENTS

The editor and publishers have made every reasonable effort to contact the copyright holders of the poems contained herein. If any involuntary infringement of copyright has occurred, sincere apologies are offered and the owners of such copyright are requested to contact the publishers.

Grateful acknowledgment is made to the following for permission to reproduce copyrighted material:

Eavan Boland for 'This Moment' from *Collected Poems* published by Carcanet Press copyright Eavan Boland 1995; Watershed Books, 71 Fermanagh Avenue, Toronto for 'When All Is Said And Done' by Lucy Brennan, copyright Lucy Brennan 1999; Dedalus Press for 'Tibetan Shepherd Boys' from *The Nitpicking of Cranes* by Paddy Bushe, copyright Paddy Bushe and The Dedalus Press 2004; Summer Palace Press for Don Byrne's 'Ouzo Time' from *Soft Shoes and Sunshine* by Don Byrne, copyright Don Byrne 2004; 'The Mirror in the Front Hall' from *The Complete Poems of Cavafy*, copyright 1961 and renewed 1989 by Rae Dalven, reprinted by kind permission of Harcourt Inc.; Billy Collins for 'The Dead' by Billy Collins from *Taking Off Emily Dickinson's Clothes* (Macmilan), copyright Billy Collins; The Estate of Padraic Colum for 'An Old Woman of the Roads' by Padraic Colum; Dedalus Press for 'On the Rooftops Rome' by Padraig J Daly; Carcanet Press for 'The Present' by Greg Delanty from *The Ship of Birth*, copyright Greg Delanty 2004; Noel Duffy for 'Daisy-Chain' by Noel Duffy from *The Silence After* published by South Tipperary Arts Centre and Start Magazine, copyright Noel Duffy 2003; Paul Durcan for 'The Cabinet Table' by Paul Durcan from *A Snail in My Prime, New and Selected Poems*, Harvill Press 1993; 'Begin' by Brendan Kennelly from *Familiar Strangers: New & Selected Poems* 1960-2004 (Bloodaxe Books, 2004); 'Wet Evening in April' by Patrick Kavanagh by kind permission of the Trustees of the Estate of the late Katherine B. Kavanagh, through the Jonathan Williams Literary Agency; Joe Kane for 'The Boy Who Nearly Won The Texaco Art Competition' copyright Joe Kane 2004; Salmon Publishing for Anne Le Marquand Hartigan's 'Cup' from *Return Single*, Beaver Row Press, copyright Anne Hartigan 1986 and Salmon Publishing; Salmon Publishing for Joan McBreen's 'Portrait of Parents and Child' from *Winter In The Eye, New & Selected Poems*, Salmon Books, copyright Joan McBreen 2003; Paula Meehan's 'The Pattern' reprinted by very kind permission of Gallery Press from *The Man Who Was Marked By Winter*, Gallery Press, Oldcastle, County Meath, copyright Paula Meehan 1991; Adrian Mitchell's 'Celia Celia' from *Heart on the Left*, reprinted by permission of PFD on behalf of Adrian Mitchell, copyright Adrian Mitchell 1997 (Adrian Mitchell Educational Health Warning: Adrian Mitchell asks that none of his poems be used in connection with any examinations whatsoever!); Bradshaw Books for 'Watching Stars' from *Some Other Country*, copyright John O'Donnell 2002; 'Years After' is taken from *Dennis O'Driscoll: New and Selected Poems* published by Anvil Press Poetry in 2004; 'Red Roses' by Anne Sexton reprinted by permission of PFD on behalf of The Estate of Anne Sexton; 'Waking' by Eileen Sheehan from *Song of the Midnight Fox* (Doghouse, May 2004, reprinted December 2004) reprinted by kind permission of Eileen Sheehan and Doghouse Publishing; 'Snowy Morning' by Henry Shukman from *Dr No's Garden* by Henry Shukman, published by Jonathan Cape, reprinted by permission of The Random House Group Ltd; Wesleyan University Press, Middleton, CT for 'A Blessing' by James Wright from *Above the River: The Complete Poems*; A P Watt Ltd on behalf of Michael B Yeats for 'The Lake Isle of Innisfree' by William Butler Yeats from *The Collected Poems* of W B Yeats, published by Macmillan.